Tasmania
AUSTRALIA

Steve Parish™
PUBLISHING

Contents

Pages 2 and 3: *Strahan is painted by sunrise colours.*   Pages 4 and 5: *Russell Falls framed by tree ferns, Mount Field National Park.*
Page 6, opposite: *Sulphur-crested Cockatoo.*   *Above: Tasmanian Waratah,* Telopea truncata.

Top: *Clouds mirrored in blue sea, Coles Bay.*   Centre: *A charming cottage and garden, Richmond.*
Above: *Green fields beneath the shadow of rugged Mount Roland.*

Introduction

Tasmania, the smallest of Australia's States, was settled some 35 000 years ago by Aboriginal people who walked across the land bridge that joined it to the rest of the continent. Around 10 000 years ago, at the end of an Ice Age, the land bridge was flooded and Tasmania became an island separated from the mainland by Bass Strait. After 1803, the British founded settlements in what was then called Van Diemen's Land. They found, to their delight, that the island's mild climate allowed them to grow familiar Northern-Hemisphere plants, and that the grazing lands were ideal for sheep and cattle. They also took seals and whales from the surrounding seas, exploited the fine timbers of the island's abundant forests and set up penitentiaries for convicts transported from England.

The island has a rich history and one of its great attractions is that, in many places, nineteenth-century buildings, and indeed entire towns, have survived in much their original condition. Splendid public buildings, houses and gardens give glimpses of life in colonial times; the places where convicts laboured under brutality and longed for freedom and escape from isolation convey the underside of colonial life.

However, for many people Tasmania's chief glory is its magnificent natural heritage. Today World Heritage listing covers one-fifth of the island, with the national parks of the south-west and west the jewels in its crown of protection. Four of these parks – Southwest, Franklin–Gordon Wild Rivers, Cradle Mountain–Lake St Clair and Walls of Jerusalem – fulfil the given definition of wilderness as a landscape "undisciplined by human hand... untouched by any need except its own evolution".

As befits an island with rich marine resources, fertile soils and temperate climate, Tasmania produces seafood and farm produce of unsurpassed quality. Much is exported to the mainland and the world, but meats, fish and crustaceans, fruits, vegetables, beers and wines form the basis of local gourmet cuisines.

Indeed, Tasmanians have brought hospitality to a fine art. The traveller can be sure of welcoming accommodation, delightful rural landscapes, unequalled wild scenery, splendid beaches and well-preserved historic buildings. Distances between places of interest are short compared with those on the mainland; every kilometre is full of fascinating sights; every destination is a place to linger, explore and savour the uniquely Tasmanian lifestyle.

Hobart

Tasmania's capital, Hobart, is Australia's most southerly city. Spreading either side of the Derwent River, sheltered from bracing westerly winds by 1270-metre Mount Wellington, it is a traveller's delight of historic buildings, beautiful gardens, intriguing places to visit and friendly, welcoming people.

Settled from Sydney in 1804 after Risdon Cove was established in 1803, Hobart Town was for many years a roaring port, where seal skins and whale oil were manhandled into ships' holds together with fine wool, grain and hides. Today, this intriguing city showcases its heritage while remaining a thoroughly modern metropolis. Battery Point's historic charms and Wrest Point Casino's sophisticated challenges are only two of Hobart's attractions.

Top: *Hobart seen from Wrest Point Casino.*
Right: *Hobart with snow-frosted Mount Wellington in the background.*

A maritime city

Situated on the deepwater estuary of the Derwent River, with easy access to the rich waters of the Tasman Sea, Hobart is a seafarers' city. The focus of the waterfront is Franklin Wharf, whose Constitution and Victoria Docks, Elizabeth Street Pier and Princes Wharf are noted for their fishing fleets. These maritime landmarks also play an important part in the festivities celebrating yachting's Sydney-to-Hobart Race in late December and February's Royal Hobart Regatta.

Harbour cruises are popular ways of seeing the natural beauty of Hobart's setting. However, for many people the high point of any visit to Tasmania's capital is dining at one of the world-class seafood restaurants on the waterfront.

Left: *An aerial view of Hobart and the River Derwent with the Tasman Bridge in the background.* Above: *(top) A replica of the brig* Lady Nelson *in Sullivans Cove; (bottom) Bellerive Marina.*

Top: *Commercial fishing boats moored in Victoria Dock in the heart of Hobart's vibrant waterfront precinct.*
Above, left and right: *Sturdy fishing craft find safe harbour at Hobart's Sullivans Cove docks.*

Above, left and right: *Pots on the decks of vessels in Victoria Dock, designed to trap the succulent crayfish, or rock lobsters, of Tasmania's coast.*

Historic Hobart

In the early 1800s, England and France were at war. Hobart was settled to prevent a possible French takeover of Van Diemen's Land, as Tasmania was then called. Fortifications and emplacements of gun batteries reflected those faraway rivalries. However, in time the thriving port's commercial connections, first with sealing and whaling, then with fishing and marine trade, led to the construction of enduring maritime warehouses, commercial properties and housing.

Today, Hobart's Battery Point is unequalled in Australia for its authentic nineteenth-century buildings and exquisite gardens. A walk there is a stroll through history. A short walk down Kelly's Steps leads to Salamanca Place, where galleries, workshops, studios and boutiques occupy the bond warehouses built between 1830 and 1850. The city is full of historic places – nearly 60 National-Trust-classified buildings in Davey and Macquarie Streets alone. The Theatre Royal (1837) is Australia's oldest, while the Cascade Brewery, established in 1824, built in 1832, still produces beer.

Above: Elegant period lamps, beautifully preserved cottages and colourful olde-worlde gardens add to the magical atmosphere of Battery Point.

Top: *Kangaroo Bluff Battery, completed in 1884.* Above left to right: *the Shipwright's Arms Hotel is a stroll from Battery Point; Cascade Brewery, Australia's oldest brewery, and still active; the colour of Saturday's Salamanca Place Markets.*

Top: *The view from the summit of Mount Wellington, once a volcanic peak.*
Above, left and right: *A lookout on Mt Wellington protects the viewer from the elements; the vista from the lookout.*

View from the summit

It is worth the journey to the top of Mt Wellington to see one of the world's most spectacular views – a glorious panorama of city, hinterland, river and ocean. Many people drive to the summit while the adventurous go on foot, but all find the scenery breathtaking. No less fascinating are the alpine plants that clothe the mountain top, and the houses perched in the trees on the lower slopes. A lookout gives some shelter in less clement weather, but there are days when cloud veils the mountain, hiding the city from view. Hobart's other, less lofty protector, Mt Nelson, may repay a visit on such occasions.

The Royal Botanical Gardens

Situated in the Queen's Domain on the western bank of the River Derwent, the Royal Tasmanian Botanical Gardens were established in 1818 as the garden of Government House. From 1828, the gardens' superintendent, William Davidson, planted formal English gardens while initiating a collection of local plants.

Today, the 13.5-hectare site boasts 6500 species and varieties of plants, including more than 400 from Tasmania, and has the Southern Hemisphere's largest public collection of conifers. A captivating Conservatory, Japanese garden and French fountain, seasonally changing floral displays, herb garden and Antarctic plant house are only a few of the many fascinating features of these spectacular gardens. Quieter moments can be spent at the Botanical Discovery Centre's interactive displays. A Tulip Festival is held in the gardens each September.

Left: *The lily pond in the Royal Tasmanian Botanical Gardens.*
Top: *The fountain in the Conservatory.* Above: *Part of the sweetly perfumed and brilliantly coloured exotic orchid display.*

The Derwent Valley

The valley of the Derwent River runs north-west of Hobart, through fertile green pastures and towns such as New Norfolk and Hamilton.

Since the 1860s, the valley has supplied hops for Australia's finest beers. The old oast houses used for drying the hops are everywhere, and the hop fields are marked out by windbreaks of poplars. Autumn, when the hops are harvested, is a colourful time to visit the valley.

The Oast House at Tynwald Park, on the Hobart side of New Norfolk, holds interesting displays of hops cultivation and processing.

Left: *Kentdale Oast House.*
Above: *Peaceful pastures overlook Bushy Park.*

Derwent Valley towns

Exploring the towns of the Derwent Valley brings to mind the fact that a journey itself is often as enjoyable as reaching the destination. These delightful rural centres lie on the routes to stunning national parks and wilderness areas, but they are well worth taking time to explore.

New Norfolk, where convict-turned-police-constable Denis McCarty built a home in 1808, was named by immigrants from the Pacific island penal colony. It was threatened by bushrangers soon afterwards. Today, the busy Australian Newsprint Mills stand nearby. At Plenty, just north-west of New Norfolk, are the delightful gardens of the Salmon Ponds, where fish imported from England in the 1860s became the progenitors of the salmon and trout so eagerly sought in Tasmanian rivers by today's fishers.

Further along the Lyell Highway from New Norfolk, on the southern edge of Tasmania's central plateau, lies historic Hamilton, a quiet nineteenth-century town set in picturesque pastoral country.

Top: *Cottages in Hamilton (left) and New Norfolk (right) that have been restored for holiday accommodation.*
Above: *Nineteenth-century cart, New Norfolk.*

Top left: *Glass memorabilia, Hamilton.*   Top right: *Victoria's Cottage, Hamilton, built by convicts in 1845.*
Above: *Glen Clyde House, a coaching inn dating to the 1840s, Hamilton.*

Mount Field National Park

The road from New Norfolk that runs along the southern bank of the Derwent River, through Plenty and Westerway, leads to Mount Field National Park, where multiple aspects of Tasmania's glorious wild areas have been preserved since 1916.

Some of the park's most notable features are easily accessible. Quite near the entrance, the spectacle of Russell Falls plunging in tiers amidst emerald-green ferns rewards a short stroll. More energetic adventurers may care to venture along the Tall Trees Circuit to Lady Barron Falls, or trek along the ridges to the rugged beauty of the Rodway Range and Tarn Shelf.

Walkers should remember always that Tasmanian weather is changeable. At any time of year, the explorer who sets out in sunshine may find halfway through the day that mist and rain have drifted in and that temperatures have dropped rapidly. Any bushwalker should carry additional warm and, if possible, rainproof clothing. The mere fact that it is available may well mean it will never be needed.

Above: *Horseshoe Falls, an easily reached highlight of Mount Field National Park.*

Top: *Tree ferns frame the crystal cascade of Russell Falls.*
Above, left to right: *Falling water, verdant foliage; Lake Dobson; alpine* Richea sprengeloide; *a Mount Field cameo.*

The Huon Valley

South-west of Hobart, the broad Huon River flows through fertile valleys that once were sheltered by towering Huon Pine. These were cut for their valuable and aromatic timber, and their place was taken by apple orchards. Today, other fine fruits and vineyards flourish in the valley and Atlantic salmon are farmed. The valley's restaurants are noted for their innovative use of fresh local produce.

The town of Geeveston is still a centre for the timber industry. The Huon River is a focus for recreational craft and fishing, and a jet-boat ride through its rapids is a memorable experience. Franklin, oldest town on the river, has a noted rowing course.

Opposite, top: *Huonville and the Huon Valley from the south.*
Opposite, far left: *Handcrafted clinker dinghies.* Left: *Franklin
Jetty, Huon River.* Above, top: *Ma Pippin's Restaurant,
Geeveston.* Centre: *Sailing boats on the Huon*
Bottom: *The Bears Went over the Mountain, Geeveston.*

Tahune AirWalk

North-west of Geeveston and 70 kilometres south-west of Hobart, Tahune Forest Reserve is found by travelling the Arve Road Forest Drive. A special feature of this reserve is the AirWalk, a sturdy, soaring steel structure that gives intimate glimpses of the forest canopy and stunning views of the Huon and Picton Rivers.

The AirWalk, like so many of Tasmania's popular natural attractions, is accompanied by an excellent interpretive centre, where visitors can learn about the unique forests surrounding them.

Above, top: *Suspended in the rainforest canopy on the AirWalk.*
Centre: *Luxuriant green tree ferns.* Bottom: *The AirWalk spans 500 metres.* Right: *Tahune Forest AirWalk soars across the forest canopy, up to 45 metres above the ground.*

Top: *Southport, a delightful seaside town on a beautiful bay.*   Centre: *An intriguing mural, Dover.*
Bottom: *Looking across Dover jetty, Port Esperance Bay and D'Entrecasteaux Channel to South Bruny Island.*

Southport and Dover

Dover, on Port Esperance, overlooking three small islands named Faith, Hope and Charity, is a seaside gem 21 kilometres south of Geeveston on the Huon Highway. Once a timber town, Dover is now home to a thriving Atlantic salmon industry, with busy fish farms and several processing plants.

South of Dover, through orchards and forests, the Hastings Forest Tour takes in tall timber, Newdegate Cave in the Hastings Caves and the Thermal Pool. Southport, at the end of the Huon Highway, was once known as "Bay of Mussels". Today's peaceful scenes contrast with the violence of the shipwrecks of the nineteenth century, the worst being in 1835 when *George III* sank just south-east of Southport with the loss of 133 souls, nearly all of them convicts who were locked below decks.

Top: *The Dover Hotel on the Huon Highway.*   Above: *Sunset over Port Esperance Bay.*

Historic Richmond

Only 20 minutes drive north-east of Hobart, the village of Richmond is a showcase for Tasmania's early history and an advertisement for the island's twenty-first century hospitality. At first glance, this town on the Coal River has been frozen in time, with its immaculate Georgian homes, two of Australia's oldest surviving churches (St Luke's and St John's, both dating to the 1830s) and the convict-built Richmond Bridge, begun in 1823. This bridge was built to connect Hobart with the Tasman and Forestier Peninsulas, and tales are told of its haunting by the ghost of a cruel overseer who was murdered by the convicts he drove so relentlessly.

Today's Richmond is a place of prim but inviting cottages, impressive public buildings and a wealth of places in which to stay, eat and enjoy the locals' hospitality. Bridge Street is lined with historic buildings, while Richmond Gaol brings memories of the convict days and the scale model of Old Hobart Town in the 1820s cannot fail to engage anyone with an interest in the colony's early days.

Top, left and right: *A scene in historic Richmond; the Richmond Arms dates to 1829.*
Above, left and right: *Restored heritage cottages in Richmond.* Opposite: *Richmond Bridge on the Coal River, and St John's Church.*

Above: *Tasman Peninsula.*

The Tasman Peninsula

Scenically memorable and historically fascinating, the Tasman Peninsula extends into the Tasman Sea, joined to island Tasmania by the 100-metre-wide isthmus called Eaglehawk Neck. When Port Arthur was a feared place of punishment for re-offending convicts, fierce dogs guarded this causeway. For some inmates, death may have seemed preferable to the "Model Prison" where prisoners lived and worked in total silence. From 1830 to 1877, about 12 000 convicts passed through Port Arthur – many remained there on the tiny Isle of the Dead in Port Arthur itself.

The Tasman Peninsula has 300-metre-high sheer cliffs, peaceful beaches such as Pirates Bay, the intriguing Tessellated Pavement and, most spectacular on a stormy day, the ocean-born violence of the Blowhole and the Devil's Kitchen.

Fortescue Bay, with its delightful sandy beach bordered by forest, is one of the best places on the peninsula to spend a lazy day relaxing while energetic sight-seers take in the coastal sights along the walking track to Cape Hauy.

Above: *The Tessellated Pavement, Eaglehawk Neck.*

Top: *Convict quarters, the Penitentiary, Port Arthur Historic Site.*
Above: *The Guard Tower and remains of the Military Barracks, Port Arthur.*

Above: *The ruins of the Chapel, gutted by fire in 1884.*

High and wild

A triangle within the greater triangle that is Tasmania, the central plateau is a region of undulating pastures, grazing flocks and myriads of lakes, great and small. To the north and coastwards, this highland drops down over the mountains called the Western Tiers.

The southern edge is defined by the Derwent River valley, and travellers following its line along the Lyell Highway towards Queenstown will eventually pass through the grandeur of Cradle Mountain–Lake St Clair National Park, one of the finest of Tasmania's World Heritage Areas.

Cradle Mountain first became a "scenic reserve and wildlife sanctuary" in 1922. The Cradle Mountain–Lake St Clair National Park was World-Heritage-listed in 1982. This is a rugged and mountainous region, whose landscapes range from wind-blasted dolerite rockfaces to gullies forested with eucalypts and beeches, shining tarns, open buttongrass moors and alpine herb fields. Mount Ossa (1617 metres) is Tasmania's highest peak.

Left: *In Cradle Mountain–Lake St Clair National Park.*
Above: *View south from the Lyell Highway to King William Range.*

Above: *The Artists Pool, Cradle Mountain–Lake St Clair National Park.*

Above: *A tranquil, sunny day at Lake Burbury, near Queenstown.*

Fascinating Ross

In 1812, on the road to Launceston, 117 kilometres
north of Hobart, the town of Ross was founded. It was
a coaching station, garrison town and farming centre.
Today it is a treasure of Tasmania, a town of National
Trust buildings and great historic interest.

Convict-built Ross Bridge was completed in 1836. A
stonemason, Daniel Herbert, who was transported for
highway robbery, contributed intricate decorative
carvings to the sandstone structure. He was granted
a pardon for his efforts.

Top: *The Uniting Church (1885).*   Above: *Ross Bridge (1836).*
Right: *The War Memorial at the Temptation, Recreation, Salvation
and Damnation Crossroads includes a Boer War field gun.*

Cradle Mountain

Opinions vary on whether Cradle Mountain was named after a baby's refuge or the rocker that miners used to separate gold from dross.

The lakes that abound in this wild area were carved out of solid rock by moving ice, the shells later filling with water as the glaciers melted. Cerulean Lake St Clair is Australia's deepest freshwater lake.

The Overland Track from Cradle Valley to Cynthia Bay is a wonderful walk in summer on which you can enjoy the wildflowers and the magnificence of the high country. This well-marked trail can be taken at any pace: the enterprising may take the chance to climb Cradle Mountain (which rises to 1545 metres) and enjoy the unequalled view from the summit.

This is one of the best places in Australia to see wildlife at close quarters, because many birds and mammals come to the huts and camping grounds.

Top: *Cradle Mountain.*
Right: *Dove Lake with Cradle Mountain in the background.*

Top: *Rainforest with a Pandani,* Richea pandanifolia, *in the left foreground.*
Above: *Walking trails in the National Park vary from easy to extreme.*

Above: *Lake Rodway reflects the surrounding peaks in the still air of early morning.*

The holiday coast

Sometimes known as "the Sun Coast", Tasmania's eastern seaboard enjoys much milder weather than the island's west. Glorious sandy beaches, scenic rocky headlands and seas rich in fish and crustaceans make east coast resorts favourites with holiday-makers. The towns of Orford, Triabunna, Swansea and Bicheno are set on a coast of remarkable natural beauty. Their restaurants serve seafood fresh from the boats that combines with local wines to make memorable meals.

On the southern end of the coast is Maria Island, reached by ferry from Louisville. This is a delightful place to spend a day, with magnificent scenery, great walks and all-too-tame native animals. Offshore, the giant kelp forests and sealife in the island's marine reserve attract scuba divers.

Above: *Landing a catch of crayfish at The Gulch, Bicheno*

Top: *Bicheno's Blowhole in action.* Centre: *Scuba diving in kelp at Maria Island.*
Bottom: *Looking across Waubs Bay to Peggy's Point, Bicheno.*

The Freycinet Peninsula

Once the scene of the slaughter of seals and whales, the Freycinet Peninsula is now a place to watch and enjoy the everyday lives of these creatures and their fellow mariners, the dolphins. The peninsula, a national park, is dominated by the 300-metre-high, red granite mountains known as The Hazards. Favourites with rock-climbers, they overlook the beauty of Coles Bay, which is ideal for swimming, windsurfing and water-skiing. Opposite, on the eastern side of the peninsula, lies scenic Wineglass Bay, with its semi-circular beach of silver sand bordered by sapphire and emerald sea.

Birdwatchers and nature-lovers find Freycinet National Park, formed in 1916 at the same time that Mount Field was gazetted, a paradise. In springtime and early summer its heaths are bright with wildflowers.

The peninsula can be reached easily from either Swansea or Bicheno, and the township of Coles Bay is the gateway to this world of pristine beaches, unforgettable scenery and some of the best bushwalks Tasmania offers.

Above: *Looking towards Cape Forestier from Cape Tourville lookout.* Right: *A view across Coles Bay to the cloud-topped Hazards.*
Pages 54 and 55: *Glorious Wineglass Bay, with its silver sands and crystal water.*

A land of plenty

Untouched beaches, undisturbed bushland and temperate climate make Tasmania's north-east a very pleasant place. Ben Lomond National Park, which contains Legges Tor, the island's second-highest peak, is known for the quality of its skiing.

The largest city in northern Tasmania, Launceston, was founded in 1805 and stands at the end of the deepwater channel of the Tamar River, 64 kilometres inland from Bass Strait.

The whole region is bountiful: dairy cattle and fat lambs graze the pastures; bees drone in blossoms; rows of vegetables march up and down gently sloping paddocks; fine vineyards and orchards cover the hills; cheese factories and bakeries are dotted throughout.

Top: *Ben Lomond seen across a pastoral valley.*
Right: *The* Lady Stelfox *paddlesteamer, moored near Paterson Bridge, Launceston.*

Launceston

A city of delightful parks and gardens, Launceston is planted with the deciduous trees of the Northern Hemisphere as well as with Australian natives. The formal Victorian atmosphere of City Park, the green lawns of Royal Park and the elegance of Princes Square give our third-oldest city a cosmopolitan air that is consolidated by a wealth of nineteenth-century colonial homes and public buildings. Two prime attractions are set in an old quarry by the Tamar. Penny Royal World brings history alive with working water- and windmills, a gunpowder mill and model craft, and is where the *Lady Stelfox*, which cruises Cataract Gorge on the South Esk River, moors.

Top: *Launceston seen from Arbour Park.*
Above: *A city mural of working conditions in a smelting factory.*

Top: *The view over Paterson Bridge and Launceston to Ben Lomond.*
Above, left to right: *Franklin House; Gas Company House; Albert Hall; Prince Albert Inn.*

Top: *Penny Royal World with its working cornmill.*
Bottom: *The colourful apartments of the Penny Royal Watermill Hotel.*

Top: *Sailing on the City Reach of the Tamar River.*
Bottom: *A peaceful scene on the Tamar River close to Launceston's city centre.*

The Tamar Valley

The Tamar Valley runs north-west from Launceston to Bass Strait. Highways make touring either bank easy, but the only crossing is at Batman Bridge, near Deviot. Fertile agricultural land extends the length of the valley, then west to the edge of the plateau known as the Great Western Tiers. It is 64 kilometres from Launceston to the sea, and on both sides of the Tamar are lush pastures, neatly ordered orchards and the vineyards that contribute to making this a premier wine-producing area. Most of these vineyards offer wine-tastings and cellar-door sales, and their vintages go particularly well with the local seafood and cheeses.

This is undoubtedly a place to enjoy good food and drink, to appreciate the rich land and sea that produce them, and to savour the pleasures of nature. This should include the waterbirds and seabirds that abound in this region – the Tasmanian coast is the final stopping-place for many of the waders that migrate from Siberia each year, and Little Penguins nest at many spots on the coast.

Above: *A Black Swan and cygnets float gracefully in the Tamar River.*

Top: *An Exmouth vineyard on a gentle slope bordering the River Tamar.*
Bottom: *Tamar Islands Wetlands Centre is a great place for birdwatching and photography.*

Rural Tasmania

Although Tasmania does not have the vast plains of mainland Australia, the red soils of its north are deep and rich. The island has long been famous for the quality of its wool, the abundance of its grain yields and the creaminess of its dairy produce. Generations of hardworking rural folk have cultivated their crops, flocks and herds on family farms.

Modern Tasmanian agriculture is changing. A new generation of farmers may choose to grow traditional crops such as potatoes and peas for mainland markets, but, equally, they may diversify into exotics such as pyrethrum daisies (for insecticides), opium poppies (legally grown for medicinal uses), truffles, lavender or walnuts.

Aquaculture in bays and estuaries supplies an ever-increasing demand for salmon, other fine table fishes and oysters.

Above: *Cows head for the dairy.*   Opposite top: *Sheep grazing near the Western Tiers.*   Centre: *Poppies growing near Poatina.*
Bottom: *Lavender cultivation near Scottsdale.*

Above and right: *Some of the historic farm buildings at Woolmers Estate, near Longford, just south of Launceston.*

Established by William Thomas Archer in 1816, this property gives glimpses into Tasmania's rural history.

Top: *Woolmer's Estate farmhouse, a delightful Italianate building.* Centre, left and right: *Store at Woolmer's Estate; a cottage window in nearby Longford.* Bottom: *Gallery and antique shop, Evandale, just south of Launceston.*

Above: *A window display at the Evandale Tinker Shop. Across the road is the Clarendon Arms.*

Liffey Forest Reserve

The rivers and streams that flow down the Great Western Tiers tumble over rocky ledges in cascades such as Liffey Falls in the Liffey Forest Reserve, a short drive south of the heritage town of Deloraine. There are actually three separate falls, and they can all be viewed after walking well-marked trails. Tasmania's rainforests are unique, and this reserve is a place to wonder at the towering tree-ferns and majestic trees, their canopies held aloft in the clear mountain air.

The quiet explorer may catch a glimpse of one of Australia's most famous but elusive creatures, the Platypus, paddling in a quiet reach of the river or diving to fossick amongst the rocks for yabbies, frogs and other tasty aquatic tidbits.

Left, opposite: *The beautiful Liffey Falls, Liffey Forest Reserve.*
Top: *Streams and ferns.* Bottom: *Platypus swimming in the sunshine.*

Sealife

The cold waters of the Southern Ocean carry drifts of microscopic plants and animals to the seas off Tasmania. This marine smorgasbord forms the base of a food triangle at whose apex are whales, seals, sea-lions, dolphins and sharks. Smaller but equally fascinating sea creatures abound, and scuba-diving is a major sport, mainly off the east coast and around the Bass Strait islands.

Seahorse farming is a novel industry that may help satisfy demand for these animals in traditional oriental medicine, which is taking them from the wild and endangering them in many parts of the world.

Above and top right: Australian Fur-seals in kelp forests off Bridport Island. *Right, from left:* A colourful seastar; Big-belly Seahorse; Six-spine Leatherjacket.

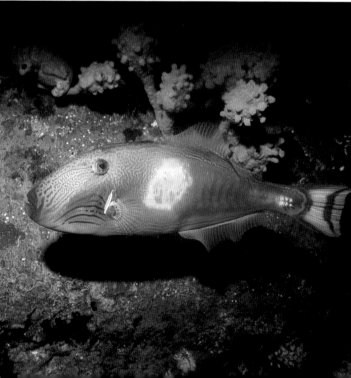

To wilder climes

Many people arrive in Tasmania at Devonport, where the Bass Strait ferry makes landfall. Bass Highway will take them westward along the coast, past Burnie with its paper mill and Wynyard where vivid tulips paint the fields in springtime. This is an area for dairy produce, vegetables and deer farms, the coast bright with sandy beaches and blue waters that shade to grey in storms.

The north-west coastal towns were founded where river estuaries made good harbours for craft bringing supplies for settlers and carrying away timber. Inland, forests have given way to farms, except in the wildest areas of mountains and gorges where many people hope that perhaps the elusive Thylacine still roams.

Opposite, left: *Lighthouses abound – this one's at Stanley.*
Top: *Table Cape Lighthouse.*
Bottom: *On a deer farm at Table Cape.*

The penguins of Penguin

The Little Penguin stands knee-high to a human adult. Its back is steel-blue and its belly silver-white, it has flippers instead of wings, and it moves on land with a sailor-like, rolling waddle. In the ocean, this bird is speed and grace personified, flashing through the water to gulp down fish and squid.

Adapted to the ocean as it is, the Little Penguin must still come to land to breed. Along Tasmania's northern coast are numbers of penguin rookeries, some in remote places and some near human dwellings. The town of Penguin, at the foot of the Dial Range, was named after the birds that attract so many people to watch them "parade" up the beach at dusk, bringing fish to their fluffy nestlings, impatiently waiting in nest burrows to be fed.

Above: *Rocky Cape National Park.*   Right (clockwise from top left): *Mersey Bluff, Devonport; Railway embankment, Penguin; Big Penguin at Penguin; Little Penguins.*

Stanley

Established in 1826, Stanley shelters beside a 150-metre rock formation that was first called Circular Head, but is now known as the Nut. A chairlift runs to the Nut's summit, and those who take advantage of it have a fine view of the surrounding land and sea.

For 30 years the town was the headquarters of the Van Diemen's Land Company, which by the 1850s had fallen on hard times and sold most of its land. The area then found new life, supplying mutton, beef and vegetables to Victoria's roaring goldfields. Its continuing prosperity was made certain by the growth of the dairy industry and the discovery of tin in the area.

Top: *The Hon. J.A. Lyons was born in 1879 in Lyon's Cottage, Church Street. He was Prime Minister of Australia from 1932 to 1939.*
Bottom: *The main street of Stanley.*

Top: *Fishing boats in Stanley Harbour.* Bottom left: *Remains of the convict barracks at Highfield with the Nut beyond.*
Right: *Highfield House, built in 1832 by the Van Diemen's Land Company.* Pages 80 and 81: *Angus cattle grazing above Stanley.*

Towards the Tiers

Many ranges such as the Great Western and Cluan Tiers rise from Tasmania's northern coastal plain. At the edge of the Central Plateau, their rugged slopes and cliffs are fissured by forested gorges. Rivers flowing from the heights attracted early settlers and today the foothills are studded with farms and towns. Sheffield, south of Devonport, is surrounded by some of Tasmania's prettiest country, graced with names such as Paradise, Beulah and the Promised Land. The land is dominated by Mount Roland (1234 metres), and nearby Lake Barrington is a big rowing venue.

The citizens of Sheffield have decorated their town with murals so that it is an outdoor art gallery. With flair, an eye to effect and considerable skill, the colourful walls of Sheffield invite passers-by to stay awhile in this idyllic place. The murals depict themes as diverse as early local history, wildlife, the charge of the Light Horse, a printer's press in action, a mountain rescue and a blacksmith's forge.

Top: *A Sheffield mural that captures the scenery around Mount Roland.*

Top: *View south from Sheffield towards Mount Roland.*
Bottom, left to right: *Peaceful pastures and Mount Roland; an old wagon at the chairmaker's gallery in West Kentish.*

Sheffield's streets are bright with restored buildings adorned with colourful murals.

Above: *The Blacksmith Gallery Antique Shop, Sheffield.*

Western wilderness

Until 1932 when the Lyell Highway was completed, the only way for people and goods to reach the west coast of Tasmania was across the often-stormy sea. Today the west is a place of enormous contrasts. Small sections rich in minerals have been heavily mined, while huge areas remain as wilderness, protected by World Heritage listing. This region has high rainfall, rushing rivers, almost impenetrable forests and towering mountains. It brings nature-lovers and adventure-seekers from all over the world. Strahan, the only port on the coast, lies in the shelter of Macquarie Harbour and is reached through the narrow opening called Hell's Gate. From Strahan, expeditions head off up the Gordon River and to many wild places.

Opposite, top: *Strahan at sunrise.*
Bottom: *The Gordon River in the early light.*
Above: *On the Gordon River.*

Queenstown

For many years Queenstown's deforested hillslopes have held a perverse attraction for photographers and visitors. Now good conservation practices are restoring growth to the landscape. The discovery of tin in 1879 and gold in 1881 brought miners to the area; then they struck silver and copper. Copper mining continues at Mount Lyell mine, though on a reduced scale.

The history of Queenstown can be discovered at the town's Gallery Museum. Tours explore the open-cut mine workings and Mining Museum, and an historic local railway is again in working order.

Above, top: *Rack and Pinion Steam Railway Station.*
Bottom: *The ABT Wilderness Railway Steam Train.*
Opposite, right: *The main street of Queenstown.*

COFFEE LOUNGE

POST OFFICE 7467

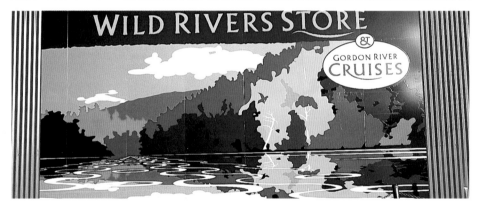

Strahan

Today, Strahan is a fishing town that serves as a jump-off point for visitors exploring the wild west coast and its memorable natural attractions. Once it was a booming port through which, first, valuable Huon pine, and then gold, silver and copper ores were exported. In 1822, a penal settlement was established on Sarah Island, the convicts working 12 hours a day to cut and saw pine trees.

Strahan boasts an impressive Customs House that is home to a World Heritage visitor centre. The Strahan Wharf Centre displays many aspects of the social and natural history of Tasmania's west and south-west.

Above, top: *Shops and galleries on Strahan's main street.*
Centre: *Old Customs House.* Bottom: *Wild Rivers Store on Strahan's wharf.*

Above, top to bottom: *Strahan wharves in the early morning sunshine.*

Top: *Mount Sorell from Sarah Island.*   Bottom left: *A cruise boat based at Strahan.*   Right: *Stormbreaker under sail.*

Macquarie Harbour

In 1815, Captain James Kelly set out to circumnavigate Tasmania in a whaleboat, with the aim of discovering natural resources. After he successfully navigated the difficult entrance to a spacious harbour, he was pleased to note that the surrounding land was covered with stately Huon pine. A year later, coal was found in the area and Lieutenant Governor Sorell began planning to establish a settlement for re-offending convicts on the harbour.

After two hundred years, Macquarie Harbour has come into its own as a place appreciated for its natural beauty rather than for its exploitable resources. Cruises from Strahan allow passengers to marvel at the lush temperate rainforests of the Franklin–Gordon Wild Rivers National Park. Flights by seaplane give a novel view of the harbour, hinterland and coast. This region is a paradise for sailing, bushwalking, fishing and "simply messing about in boats".

Top left: *Cray fishermen at Hell's Gates near Cape Sorell Lighthouse.*   Right: *Bonnet Island Lighthouse, Macquarie Harbour entrance.*
Bottom left: Lady Woodward *fish farm.*   Right: *Colourful fishing shacks at Lettes Point.*

Sarah Island

The penal colony at Sarah Island on Macquarie Harbour was established in 1822 as a place of punishment for the "worst description of convicts" in Van Diemen's Land. Convicts survived on scanty rations and forced labour, cutting and sawing Huon pine and mining coal. They were flogged or subjected to solitary confinement for small offences. Over 180 escape attempts were made (one group of escapees reached Chile) and murders and suicides were common. Sarah Island penitentiary was closed in 1833 and the island later became a base for timber-getters.

By the end of the 1800s, the ruins of Sarah Island attracted day-trippers: in 1926 the island was gazetted as a tourist reserve, and was declared an Historic Site in 1971. Finally, with nearby Grummet Island, it was included in the Tasmanian Wilderness World Heritage area.

Today Sarah Island and the derelict timber and mining town of Pillinger are reminders of past times of savagery and hard labour.

Above: *Relics of habitation near the derelict township of Pillinger, Kelly Bay.*

Ruins on Sarah Island. Top: *Remains of the penitentiary.* Bottom left: *Steps of the old bakery.* Right: *A brick kiln.*

Above: *On the lower reaches of the Gordon River.*

Wild Rivers

In the 1950s the Tasmanian Hydro-Electricity Commission decided to harness the wild rivers of the State's south-west for power. The Huon and Gordon Rivers were dammed in 1972, flooding Lake Pedder, but conservationists rallied from all over the world to save the Franklin from a like fate. With Commonwealth intervention, dam construction was stopped, and, in 1982, the Franklin–Gordon Wild Rivers National Park was listed as a World Heritage Area.

Much of the park is covered by thick rainforest growing on steep mountain slopes. For the daring, white-water rafting down the Franklin is a way to see one of the world's wildest areas. Less physically taxing, but no less satisfying, is a river cruise from Strahan up the Gordon to Heritage Landing.

Above left: *Nelson Falls, just west of Lake Burbery, in Franklin–Gordon Wild Rivers National Park.*
Right: *Rainforest in Franklin–Gordon Wild Rivers National Park.*

Southwest National Park

The eastern boundary of Southwest National Park is only about 100 kilometres west of Hobart. It is a remarkable experience to fly across the cultivated landscape surrounding Tasmania's capital, then soar over the majestic mountains and impenetrable forest of country almost untouched by human activities.

There are few roads into the south-west and those who wish to explore Tasmania's largest national park had better be well-prepared and self-sufficient. These landscapes emerged at the end of the last Ice Age, with rugged peaks ripped free of soil by glacial action, tarns gouged from the high plateaus by moving ice, and tangled vegetation growing below the soaring crowns of pines and eucalypts. The plant life is amazing, and often unique: in summer the meadows nestled between the mountain peaks are bright with wildflowers and alive with birds.

Left, opposite: *A tarn in the Arthur Ranges.*   Above: *Prion Bay with Precipitous Bluff in the background.*

Top: *The rugged coast at Prion Bay.*   Centre: *Lake Pedder in soft evening light.*   Bottom: *A solitary yacht in Port Davey.*

Top: *Precipitous Bluff shrouded in sea mist.*   Centre: *Sea coast near Port Davey.*
Bottom: *Tarns and craggy peaks are characteristic of the Arthur Ranges.*

Tasmania's wildflowers

Tasmania has at least 2000 species of native flowering plants. Some twenty, including the dainty Tasmanian Waratah, grow only in the Island State. Sixty species of ground orchid are found in Freycinet National Park alone. The tallest flowering plant in the world, the Swamp Gum, *Eucalyptus regnans*, which can be 100 metres high, is found in the island's forests, while another eucalypt, the Tasmanian Blue Gum, *Eucalyptus globulus*, is the State's floral emblem. This hardwood is cultivated as a source of timber in Tasmanian plantations as well as in many places overseas.

Alpine plants abound in summer in Tasmania's high country, but they are fragile and easily damaged by careless walkers. More easily seen are the wildflowers that grow along the verges of roads and in the bush, plants that bloom at their best when spring and summer bring warm sunshine that completes the work of the abundant winter rainfall.

Above: *Blossom of Tasmanian Blue Gum,* Eucalyptus globulus.

Top left: *Native Laurel*, Anopterus glandulosus.   Right: *Mountain Lilac*, Prostanthera lacianthos.   Centre left: *Showy Parrot Pea*, Dillcoynia sericea.   Right: *A peaflower*, Pultenaea speciosa.   Bottom, left to right: *Victorian Heath*, Epacris impressa; *Tasmanian Christmas Bell*, Blandfordia punicea; *Grass-leafed Triggerplant*, Stylidium graminifolium.

Above, left: *The endangered Orange-bellied Parrot.*   Right: *The migratory Swift Parrot.*

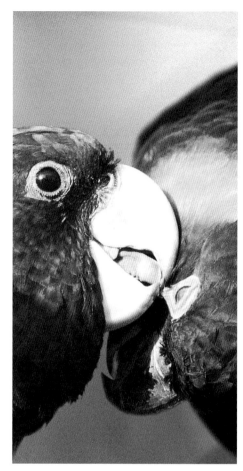

Tasmania's parrots

Of all the birds found in Tasmania, none are more colourful or endearing to humans than the parrots and cockatoos. The long separation of the island from the rest of Australia has allowed some species to change enough to be distinct from mainland birds. The Green Rosella, which can be seen in large flocks in winter in parks, gardens and heathlands, is one such endemic bird. A much more elusive feathered jewel, the Swift Parrot, breeds in Tasmania's eucalypt forests in summer, then flies across Bass Strait to spend winter on the mainland.

The entire wild population of Swift Parrots is thought to comprise only about 5000 birds, but it is outdone in rarity by the Orange-bellied Parrot. Only hundreds of these remain to breed in Tasmania's south-west wilderness, then migrate to spend winter on Victoria's coast. Urban and industrial development threaten these refuges and the parrot is listed as endangered.

Cockatoos are large, crested parrots. Tasmania is graced by the nomadic Yellow-tailed Black-Cockatoo and the spectacular Sulphur-crested Cockatoo (page 6).

Above, left: *Yellow-tailed Black-Cockatoos' courtship preening.* Right: *Tasmania's Green Rosella.*

Clockwise from top left: *Eastern Grey Kangaroo; Common Wombat; Common Brushtail Possum; Tasmanian Pademelon; Long-nosed Potoroo; Red-necked Wallaby (known as Bennett's Wallaby in Tasmania).*

Marvellous Mammals

In past ages, Tasmania was part of mainland Australia. However, around 10 000 years ago, towards the end of the last major Ice Age, meltwater caused the sea level to rise, forming Bass Strait. Tasmania's plants and animals were cut off and developed in isolation. Since the Dingo never reached the island, the unique Thylacine remained the largest predator until it was killed out by European settlers. Today, Tasmania is a sanctuary for native mammals. Some, like the Eastern Quoll, Tasmanian Devil, Tasmanian Bettong and Red-bellied Pademelon have disappeared from the mainland, while the Long-nosed Potoroo is fast following them into exile. Tragically, in the first years of the twenty-first century, some malicious person let Foxes loose in Tasmania. Unless they are eradicated, the abundant and tame small mammals of the island's bushlands may become just a memory.

Above: *Eastern Quoll with babies.*

Of tigers and devils

Early European settlers in Tasmania named the Tasmanian Devil for its terrible screech and its wide gape, full of menacing teeth. In spite of being today's largest carnivorous marsupial, the Devil stands only about 30 centimetres high at the shoulder, and looks small for the volume of noise it makes when fighting over a roadkill wallaby or other tasty meal. A female Devil carries her four young ones in a backwards-facing pouch until they are old enough to be left in a grass-lined den. The youngsters are very playful and active.

The largest carnivorous marsupial of modern times, the Thylacine, or Tasmanian Tiger, is probably now extinct. The "pouched dog with a wolf-like head" was a nocturnal predator of kangaroos and wallabies, and early farmers were quick to hunt it. The last-known Thylacine died in Hobart Zoo in 1936 – the very year that the Tasmanian Government declared the species protected. There has been no confirmed sighting since, but hope springs eternal in Thylacine-spotters' breasts.

Above, top: *A pair of Tasmanian devils.*   Bottom: *The probably extinct Tasmanian Tiger or Thylacine.*
Opposite, right: *A Tasmanian Devil in threatening/defensive mode.*

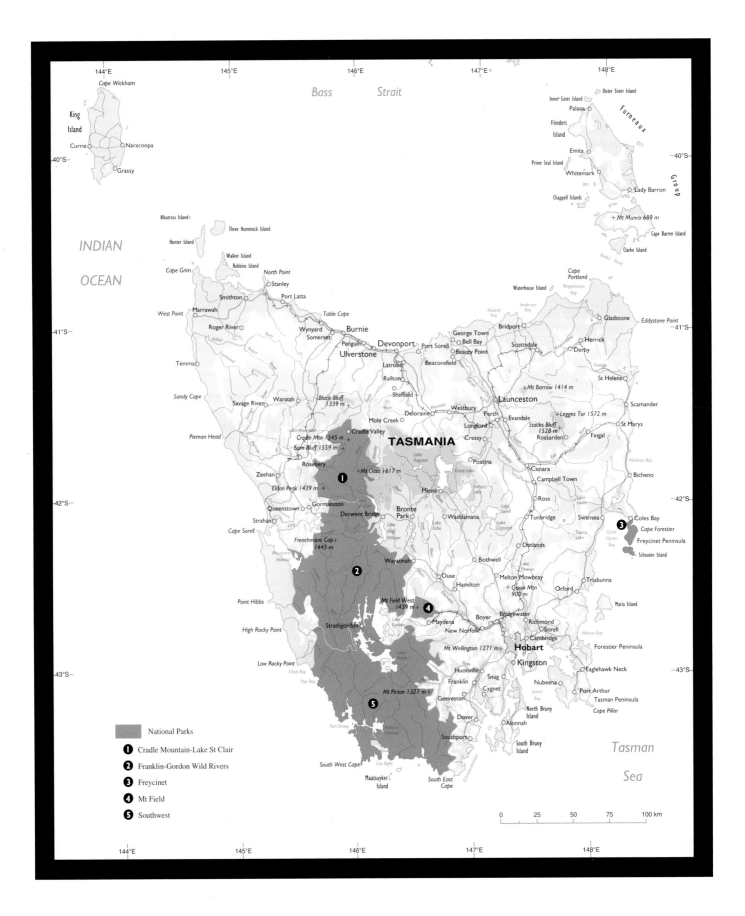

144°E 145°E 146°E 147°E 148°E

Bass   Strait

Cape Wickham

King
Island

Currie
○Naracoopa

○Grassy

−40°S

INDIAN

OCEAN

Albatross Island

Hunter Island

Cape Grim

Walker Island
Robbins Island

North Point
○Stanley
Port Latta
○Smithton

West Point
○Marrawah

Table Cape
Wynyard
Somerset
Burnie

Roger River○

○Temma

Penguin
Ulverstone
Devonport
Port Sorell
Latrobe
Beauty Point
Beaconsfield
Railton
Sheffield

George Town
Bell Bay

Bridport
Gladstone

Waterhouse Island
*Cape
Portland*

Eddystone Point

Scottsdale
Herrick
Derby

−41°S

Sandy Cape

Savage River○
○Waratah

*Black Bluff
1339 m* +

Mole Creek

Deloraine
Westbury
Perth
Longford
Cressy

St Helens

Mt Barrow 1414 m +
Launceston
Evandale

Legges Tor 1572 m +
Scamander

St Marys

*Stacks Bluff
1528 m*
Rossarden
Fingal

Pieman Head

○Rosebery

Cradle Mtn 1545 m +
Barn Bluff 1559 m +
○Cradle Valley

TASMANIA

+*Mt Ossa 1617 m*

Poatina○

Miena○

Conara
Campbell Town

Bicheno

−42°S

Zeehan○

Eldon Peak 1439 m +

❶

○Gormanston
Queenstown○
Strahan○

Derwent Bridge○

Cape Sorell

Bronte
Park○

Waddamana○

Ross○

Tunbridge

Swansea

❸ ○Coles Bay
Cape Forestier

Freycinet Peninsula

Frenchmans Cap +
1445 m

*Macquarie
Harbour*

❷

Wayatinah○

Bothwell○

Oatlands○

Schouten Island

Point Hibbs

*Mt Field West
1439 m* +

❹
○Maydena

Ouse○
Hamilton○

Melton Mowbray○
+*Quoin Mtn
900 m*
Orford○

Triabunna○

Maria Island

High Rocky Point

Strathgordon○

New Norfolk○

Boyer○
Bridgewater
Richmond○
Sorell○
Cambridge

Forestier Peninsula

Low Rocky Point

Mt Picton 1327 m +

Mt Wellington 1271 m +

Hobart
Kingston

Marion Bay

−43°S

❺

Huonville○
Franklin○
Cygnet○
Geeyeston○

Snug○

Dover○
*North Bruny
Island*
Alonnah○

Nubeena○
Port Arthur○
Tasman Peninsula
Cape Pillar

Eaglehawk Neck○

Tasman

Sea

Southport○

*South Bruny
Island*

South West Cape

*Maatsuyker
Island*

*South East
Cape*

Outer Sister Island
Inner Sister Island
○Palana

Flinders
Island

Furneaux

Emita○

Prime Seal Island
Whitemark○

○Lady Barron

Chappell Islands

+*Mt Munro 689 m*

Cape Barren Island

Clarke Island

Group

National Parks

❶ Cradle Mountain-Lake St Clair

❷ Franklin-Gordon Wild Rivers

❸ Freycinet

❹ Mt Field

❺ Southwest

0   25   50   75   100 km

Index

Published by Steve Parish Publishing Pty Ltd
PO Box 1058, Archerfield, Queensland 4108 Australia
www.steveparish.com.au
© copyright Steve Parish Publishing Pty Ltd
ISBN 1740212169
Text: Pat Slater
Map supplied by MAPgraphics, Australia
Printed in Singapore by Craft Print International Ltd
Film by Colour Chiefs, Brisbane, Queensland, Australia

Photography: Steve Parish

Additional photography: p.60, Penny Royal Gunplwder Mill, Geoff Higgens, The Photo Library; pp. 76–7, Little Penguins, Hans and Judy Beste; p. 104, Orange-bellied Parrot, Dave Watts; p. 104, Swift Parrot, Graeme Chapman.